Crafts to Make in the Fall

CRAFTS FOR ALL SEASONS

Crafts
to make
in the
Fall

KATHY ROSS

Illustrated by Vicky Enright

The Millbrook Press   Brookfield, Connecticut

For Abby, Brad, and Benj with love—K. R.

For my wonderful little boy, Sean—V. E.

Library of Congress Cataloging-in-Publication Data
Ross, Kathy (Katharine Reynolds), 1948–
Crafts to make in the Fall / by Kathy Ross ; illustrated by Vicky Enright.
p.   cm. — (Crafts for all seasons)
Summary: Presents twenty-nine easy-to-make craft projects with
autumn themes, including a fall tree lapel pin, a crow
rod puppet, and a soft sculpture pumpkin.
ISBN 0-7613-0318-9 (lib. bdg.) — ISBN 0-7613-0335-9 (pbk.)
1. Handicraft—Juvenile literature. 2. Autumn—Juvenile literature.
[1. Handicraft. 2. Autumn.] I. Enright, Vicky, ill. II. Title.
III. Series: Ross, Kathy (Katharine Reynolds), 1948– Crafts for all seasons.
TT160.R7142285   1998
745.5—dc21   97-40184   CIP   AC

Published by The Millbrook Press, Inc.
2 Old New Milford Road
Brookfield, Connecticut 06804

Contents

In many places leaves turn spectacular shades of yellow, red, and orange in the fall.

Fall Tree Lapel Pin

Here is what you need:

 four 12-inch (30-cm) brown pipe cleaners

scissors

about twenty red, yellow, and orange flat buttons

 safety pin

Here is what you do:

1 Hold three of the brown pipe cleaners together and bend them in half. Twist about 3 inches (8 cm) of the folded end of the pipe cleaners together to form a trunk for the tree. Spread the ends of the pipe cleaners out to form branches for the tree.

2 Cut the remaining pipe cleaner into 3-inch (8-cm) pieces. Wrap the pieces around the branches of the tree to make smaller branches.

3 Slide the buttons onto the different branches of the tree to look like colorful leaves.

4 Slip the back of the safety pin between the twisted pipe cleaners to form a clasp so you can wear your tree as a lapel pin.

You might want to stand the tree in a ball of clay to use as a table decoration. Be sure to tape some felt to the bottom of the clay or put a dish under it so that the moist clay does not leave a mark on the table.

7)

This tree puppet changes color just like trees do each fall.

Changing Tree Puppet

Here is what you need:

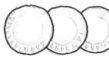 three 9-inch (23-cm) paper plates

 orange and green poster paint and a paintbrush

 orange and green tissue paper

 brown construction paper

 scissors

white glue

stapler

ruler

newspaper to work on

Here is what you do:

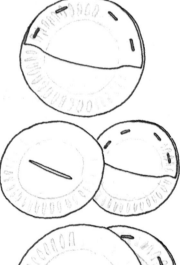

1 Cut one paper plate in half. Staple one half to the side of the second paper plate, keeping the staples around the outer edge of the plates.

2 Hold the last plate over the side of the plate with the half plate stapled to it. Cut a slit across the last plate about 1 inch (2½ cm) below the center of the plate so that your fingers will slip through the plate into the pocket formed by the half plate and the front plate. Staple the last plate in place making sure the cut is lined up with the opening to the half plate in between the two plates.

3 Turn the plates over so that the slit is across the back. Paint the front plate green. Cut lots of 1-inch (2½-cm) squares of green tissue paper. Crumple the squares and glue them over the front of the green to look like leaves. Let the paint and glue dry.

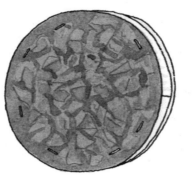

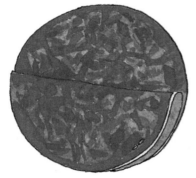

4 Fold the front, green plate down so that you can no longer see the green leaves. Paint the white plate surface orange. Cut lots of 1-inch (2½-cm) squares of orange tissue paper. Crumple the squares and glue them over the orange surface to look like leaves.

5 Cut a trunk for the tree puppet from brown construction paper. Glue the top of the trunk to the back of the tree, so it hangs down from the cut across the back of the puppet.

To use the puppet, slip your fingertips into the cut at the back of the tree. Flatten your hand to show the tree with green leaves. To change the leaves to orange, bend your fingers down to fold the green tree down and expose the orange tree.

When you do this project, you end up with two fall decorations instead of one.

Leaf Print Banner and Window Leaves

Here is what you need:

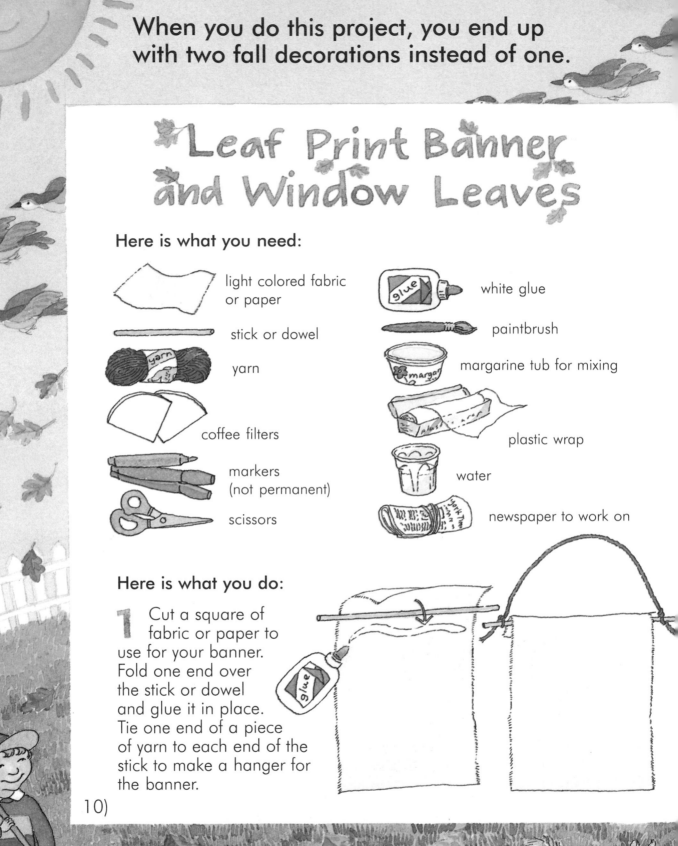

light colored fabric or paper

stick or dowel

yarn

coffee filters

markers (not permanent)

scissors

white glue

paintbrush

margarine tub for mixing

plastic wrap

water

newspaper to work on

Here is what you do:

1 Cut a square of fabric or paper to use for your banner. Fold one end over the stick or dowel and glue it in place. Tie one end of a piece of yarn to each end of the stick to make a hanger for the banner.

10)

2 Cut two or three leaf shapes from coffee filters.

3 Color the leaves with markers. You can use patches of color or layers of color to color them. Avoid using too many dark colors, because they will run into the other colors and make them muddy.

4 Mix one part glue with one part water. Paint the colored side of each leaf with this mixture.

5 Place the wet leaves one at a time, face down, on the banner. Cover the leaf with plastic wrap and rub over it to transfer the leaf pattern onto the banner. You can get at least two prints from each leaf. Cover the banner with colorful leaf prints.

Save the colored leaves. When they are dry, they will look beautiful taped on a sunny window.

11)

Nature Collection Box

Here is what you need:

 shoe box

 five zip-to-close bags

 poster paint and paintbrush

stapler

 yellow construction paper

 white glue

scissors

newspaper to work on

Here is what you do:

1 Paint the lid and the box and let them dry. You might want to make a label for the lid of the box that says your name and Nature Collection.

2 Cut a piece of construction paper to fit inside each of the plastic bags. Line each bag.

3 Cut a piece of construction paper to fit in the bottom of the box. Staple the paper to the side of one bag, stapling only the back of the bag behind the liner. Also, staple the paper along the bottom edge of the bag, through both sides of the bag.

4 Staple the side of the next bag to the side of the first bag, making sure that the bag openings face in the same direction. Staple all of the bags together to form a strip of five bags.

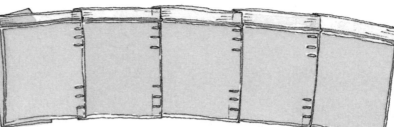

5 Cut a piece of construction paper to fit in the lid of the shoe box. Staple the piece to the side of the last bag in the row, stapling behind the liner. Also, staple the paper along the bottom edge of the bag, through both sides of the bag.

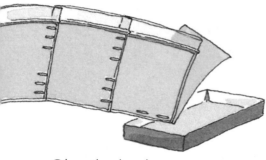

6 Glue the back paper on one end of the row of bags into the bottom of the shoe box. Glue the back paper on the other end of the row of bags into the lid of the shoe box. Let the glue dry.

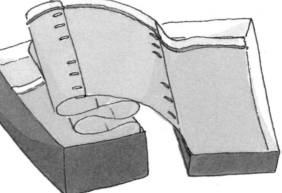

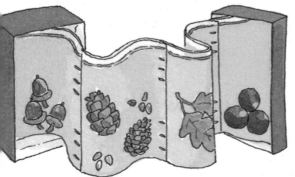

Use tape or glue to attach natural treasures such as leaves and seeds to the paper liners inside the plastic bags. To store your collection, just fold the bags, fan-style, into the shoe box. To display your collection, stand the box on one end and pull the lid out from the box to stand the bags up.

Now that you are back in school, these magnets are just what you need to help display your best work.

Handprint Magnets

Here is what you need:

 poster board

 scissors

sticky-backed magnet

poster paint and a paintbrush

 black permanent marker

Here is what you do:

1 Paint your right hand with poster paint and make a handprint on the poster board. Do the same thing with your left hand. Let the prints dry.

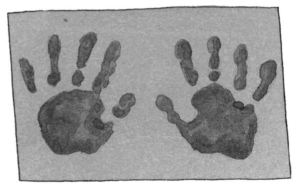

2 Cut around the outside of both handprints.

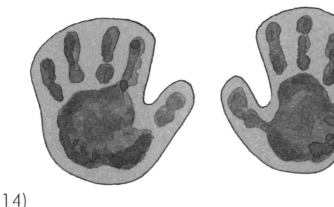

14)

3 Write the possessive form of your name on one hand and something like "work" or "masterpiece" on the other hand.

BEN'S

WORK

4 Put a piece of sticky-backed magnet on the back of each hand.

Put these handprints on your refrigerator to hold up your school and art work for all to appreciate.

15)

Make this clever picture frame to display your own school picture along with those of your friends.

School Bus Picture Frame

Here is what you need:

 empty watercolor paint box

 yellow and white construction paper

 scissors

yellow yarn

white glue

masking tape

markers

Here is what you do:

1 Trace around the paint box on the yellow paper. This will be the windows of the bus. Draw a bus shape without wheels around the windows. Cut out the bus shape. Cut out the window area of the bus shape.

2 Cut a 2-foot (60-cm) piece of yellow yarn. Open the paint box and thread the yarn inside the box around each side of the hinges. Tie the ends of the yarn together to make a hanger.

3 Close the box. Put the bus shape down over the paint box so that the box becomes windows for the bus. Turn the bus over and use masking tape to hold the bus in place around the paint box.

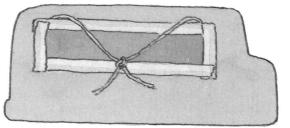

4 Cut wheels for the bus from the white paper. Glue them in place at the bottom of the bus.

5 Cut a piece of white paper to fit inside the paint box windows. Put a strip of masking tape across the bottom of the box to create a better gluing surface. Glue the white paper liner inside the box.

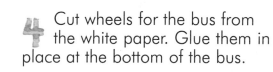

6 Use markers to decorate the bus any way you wish.

Use small pieces of rolled masking tape to tape school pictures in the paint box windows of the bus to look like passengers looking out.

17)

Make this caterpillar in the colors of the ones found in your area in the fall.

Circle Caterpillar

Here is what you need:

12-inch (30-cm) pipe cleaner

construction paper in colors you want your caterpillar to be

scissors

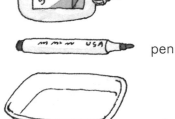

white glue

pen

Styrofoam tray

Here is what you do:

1 Cut about twenty-five 2-inch (5-cm) circles from one or more colors of construction paper.

2 Place each circle on the Styrofoam tray and use the pen to poke a small hole in the center.

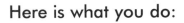

3 Thread one circle onto the pipe cleaner. Slide it almost to the end. Bend the end of the pipe cleaner up to keep the circle from sliding off.

4 To make the body of the caterpillar, slide all the circles onto the pipe cleaner, leaving a small space between each one. Leave about 3 inches (8 cm) of pipe cleaner at the head end of the caterpillar.

5 Cut a 5-inch (13-cm)-long piece of pipe cleaner. Fold the piece in half and curl the ends to make antennae for the caterpillar. Attach the antennae to the front circle of the caterpillar using the leftover pipe cleaner from the body.

6 Cut eyes from construction paper. Glue them to the front circle of the caterpillar.

Unlike the real thing, this caterpillar will stay a caterpillar.

Crow Rod Puppet

Here is what you need:

 two 2-inch (5-cm) Styrofoam balls

black yarn

corrugated box cardboard

two wiggle eyes

orange felt scrap

four black craft feathers

12-inch (30-cm) stick or dowel

white glue
scissors

Here is what you do:

1 Cut a 6-inch (15-cm) square of box cardboard. Wrap the yarn loosely around the cardboard about thirty times. Cut the wrapped yarn off the main ball of yarn.

2 Tie it together at the top by slipping a 12-inch (30-cm) piece of black yarn under the wrapped yarn and tieing it snugly around the yarn. Slide the tied yarn off the cardboard.

3 Cut the bottom of the wrapped yarn apart so that you have a big tassel of yarn tied together at the top. Work the ends of the 12-inch (30-cm) piece into the tassel.

4 Put the place where the yarn is tied on a Styrofoam ball and spread the yarn around the ball to cover it. Use a piece of black yarn to tie the yarn in place around the ball. This will be the head of the crow.

5 Place the second Styrofoam ball under the first one and tie the yarn around it. This will be the body of the crow.

6 The remaining yarn hanging down will form the tail of the crow. You may need to trim the ends a little to even them out.

7 Fold the orange felt in half. Cut a beak for the crow on the fold, so that it will have a top and bottom beak. Press the fold of the beak into the head of the crow using the end of your scissors.

8 Glue two wiggle eyes on the head. Poke a black feather into each side of the body for wings. Poke two feathers into the base of the tail above the tail yarn. Push the end of the stick into the bottom of the crow to make a handle to hold the puppet by.

Crows like to travel in flocks. You may want to make more than one crow puppet so you'll have a flock of them to tease the scarecrow puppet on the next page.

21)

If you made one or more crow puppets, you may want to make this scarecrow to keep them from becoming too big a nuisance.

Scarecrow Rod Puppet

Here is what you need:

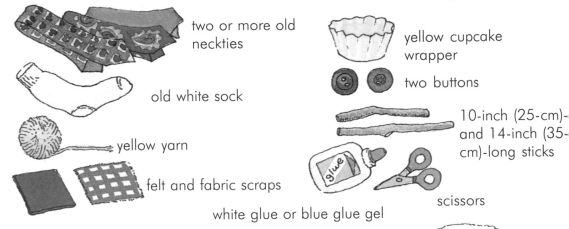

two or more old neckties

old white sock

yellow yarn

felt and fabric scraps

white glue or blue glue gel

yellow cupcake wrapper

two buttons

10-inch (25-cm)- and 14-inch (35-cm)-long sticks

scissors

Here is what you do:

1 Cut a 4-inch (10-cm) piece from the toe of the sock. Cut the rest of the sock into pieces and use them to stuff the cut toe end. This will be the head of the scarecrow. Use a piece of yarn to tie the stuffed head closed around one end of the longer stick.

2 Cut a 12-inch (30-cm) rectangle from the wide end of a tie. Fold the piece in half and cut a small slit in the center of the fold for a neck hole. Put the bottom end of the stick down into the neck hole, then slide the tie up under the head of the scarecrow to make the body.

3 Cut a 10-inch (25-cm) strip from the thin end of a tie for arms. If you keep the point, cut the other end into a point too. Slide the short stick through the tie arms to support them. Glue the arms between the top front and back of the body so that they stick out on each side of the scarecrow.

4 Cut a 12-inch (30-cm) piece from the thin end of another tie. Trim off the point. Fold the piece in the center to make a V shape. Glue the point of the V between the front and back of the bottom of the body so that the two ends of the tie piece hang down to form legs for the scarecrow.

5 Cut bits of yellow yarn for straw. Glue the yarn pieces sticking out from the bottom of the head and the ends of the arms and legs.

6 Glue the two buttons on the head of the scarecrow for eyes. Cut a triangle nose from felt and glue it on. Glue the yellow cupcake wrapper on the scarecrow's head for a straw hat.

7 Cut patches from the fabric and felt scraps. Glue them on the scarecrow.

Can your scarecrow keep those pesky crows out of the corn?   23)

Rosh Hashanah, the Jewish New Year, is celebrated in the fall.

Apple New Year Card

Here is what you need:

- two 6-inch (15-cm) paper plates
- apple seeds
- red poster paint and a paintbrush
- masking tape
- newspaper to work on
- black marker

- yellow, brown, and green construction paper
- scissors
- white glue
- hole punch
- plastic grocery bag
- yarn

Here is what you do:

1 Paint the back of both paper plates red and let them dry.

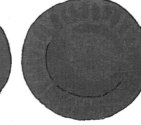

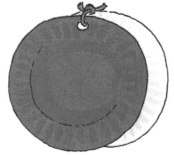

2 Stack the two plates together with the red bottoms facing out on each side, to form the front and back of an apple. Punch a hole through the edge of both plates. Tie the two plates together loosely through the holes with a piece of yarn.

24)

3 Cut a stem and leaf for the apple from the construction paper. Glue the stem and leaf to the top edge of one side of the apple so that they conceal the hole and yarn tie.

4 Cut a bee from yellow paper. Use the black marker to add details to the bee. Cut wings for the bee from the plastic grocery bag. Wrap the center of the wings with a thin piece of masking tape. Glue the taped portion of the wings to the back of the bee.

5 Open the apple card up and write a New Year's greeting inside and sign your name. Glue apple seeds down the center of the message so that the white side of the paper plate looks like the inside of an apple.

Wishing you
a sweet
New Year
Love
Ira

Make apple New Year cards for all your friends and family.

The story of Jonah and the whale is told on the Jewish holiday of Yom Kippur.

Jonah Into the Whale Flip Game

Here is what you need:

medium-size paper or plastic cup

adult-size old black sock

two wiggle eyes

hole punch

clamp clothespin

white glue

scissors

yarn

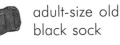

markers

Here is what you do:

1 Cut the cuff off the black sock. Cover the cup with the cuff of the sock. Pull the top of the sock about 1 inch (2½ cm) over the opening of the cut so that it forms the mouth of the whale.

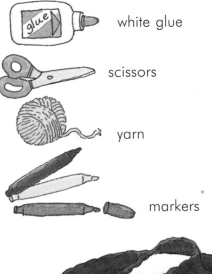

2 Cut the excess sock hanging down from the bottom of the cup into a forked shape to make a tail for the whale. Glue the top and bottom layers of the sock tail together.

3 Glue two wiggle eyes to the head of the whale above the mouth.

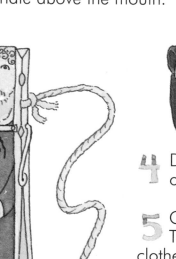

4 Draw the figure of Jonah on one side of the clothespin with markers.

5 Cut an 18-inch (45-cm) piece of yarn. Tie one end around one clamp of the clothespin. Glue the clothespin shut.

6 Punch a hole in the rim of the cup inside the sock covering and on one side of the mouth of the whale. Tie the other end of the yarn through the hole in the cup.

See if you can flip Jonah into the mouth of the whale.

When the giant sunflowers of summer start dropping seeds, you know that fall is here.

Sunflower Seeds Bowl

Here is what you need:

 sunflower seeds

 small plastic margarine tub

 white glue

 craft stick

Here is what you do:

1 Fill the tub half full of sunflower seeds.

2 Add enough white glue to completely coat all of the seeds. Use the craft stick to mix the seeds and the glue completely.

3 Shape the gluey seeds into a bowl shape by pressing seeds around the sides of the tub and flat on the bottom. Let the glue dry completely. This could take several days.

4 When the glue is dry carefully peel the seed bowl out of the margarine tub. If the bottom is still a little gluey, just turn the bowl over and let it dry.

This little bowl would make a lovely gift for someone you know.

Fall means lots of delicious apples.

Stuffed Apple

Here is what you need:

old white sock

fiberfill

red and green poster paint and a paintbrush

green felt scrap

rubber band

green yarn

scissors

hole punch

Styrofoam tray for drying

Here is what you do:

1 Cut a 5-inch (13-cm) piece from the toe end of the sock.

2 Stuff the toe with fiberfill to make a round apple shape. Close the opening of the sock with a rubber band.

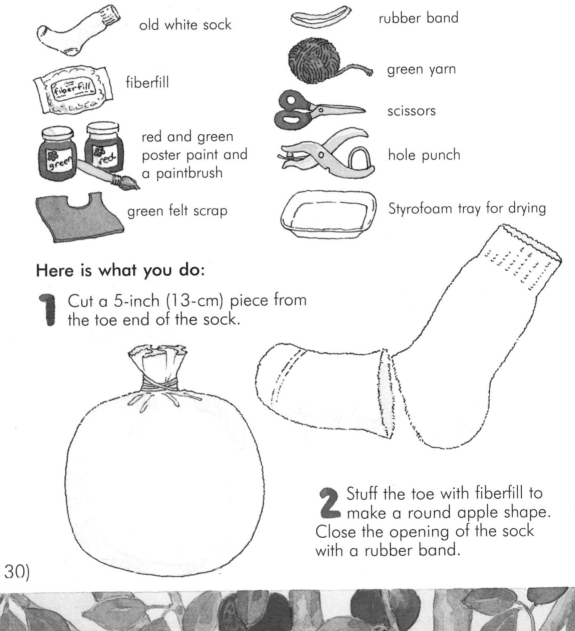

3 Paint the round part of the apple red. Paint the excess sock above the rubber band green and twist it into a stem while it is still wet.

4 Cut a leaf shape from the green felt. Punch a hole at the base of the leaf.

5 Cut an 8-inch (20-cm) piece of green yarn. Thread the leaf onto the yarn and tie it to the base of the stem of the apple. Wrap the yarn around the rubber band to conceal it. Tie the ends together to hold the leaf and yarn in place.

Make just one apple or several to display in a basket or bowl.

31)

The squirrels are noticeably busy in the autumn of the year gathering nuts to eat during the winter.

Cork Squirrel

Here is what you need:

 cork

 two small wiggle eyes

cotton ball

 tiny brown pom-pom

brown paper scrap

brown marker

scissors

white glue

Here is what you do:

1 Stretch the cotton ball out to make a tail for the squirrel. Dab the cotton with the side of the brown marker to add color. Glue the tail up one side of the cork.

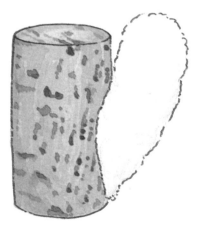

2 Glue the two wiggle eyes and the pom-pom nose to the top front of the cork.

3 Cut two pointy ears from the brown paper. Glue the ears to the front of the squirrel above the eyes.

Make a large family of squirrels using corks of varying shapes and sizes.

Columbus Day Hat

Here is what you need:

white and blue construction paper and other colors

white glue

scissors

markers

stapler

Here is what you do:

1 Cut a 2½-inch (6-cm)-wide band from the blue construction paper. Make it long enough to fit around your head. You may need to staple two bands of paper together to make a strip that is long enough. Cut the top of the band into waves so that it looks like the ocean. Staple the two ends of the band together.

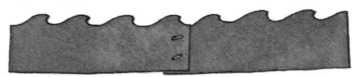

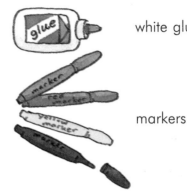

2 Cut three ships from different color papers. Label them *Niña, Pinta*, and *Santa Maria*, the names of Columbus's three ships. Cut sails for each ship from the white paper and glue them in place.

Santa Maria

Niña

Pinta

3 Glue the bottom of each ship around the inside band to look like they are sailing on the ocean.

You might want to write something on your band like "Happy Columbus Day" or the verse that helps you remember the year: "In fourteen hundred and ninety two, Columus sailed the ocean blue..."

Firefighter Down the Pole

Here is what you need:

 cardboard paper towel tube

white paper

aluminum foil

cellophane tape

 red yarn

markers

stapler

scissors

Here is what you do:

1 Cover the tube with aluminum foil to make the pole. Tuck the extra foil into each end of the tube. Use tape to hold the foil in place around the tube.

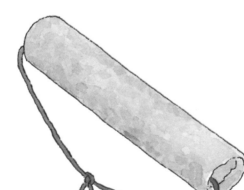

2 Cut a piece of yarn about 2½ times as long as the tube. String one end of the yarn through the tube and knot the ends together at the bottom. Leave 4 or 5 inches (10 or 13 cm) of extra yarn at each end of the tube after the knot. Make sure the yarn is loose enough so that it slides easily through the tube.

36)

3 Use the markers to draw a 4-inch (10-cm)-tall firefighter on the white paper. Cut around the firefighter picture.

4 Staple the firefighter above the yarn knot outside the tube.

To slide the firefighter down the pole, just pull on the excess yarn below the knot.

Books Bookmark

Here is what you need:

 book catalog or flyer

 yarn

 white glue

 clear packing tape

cereal box cardboard or posterboard

hole punch

scissors

Here is what you do:

1 Cut five book cover pictures from a book club flyer or catalog.

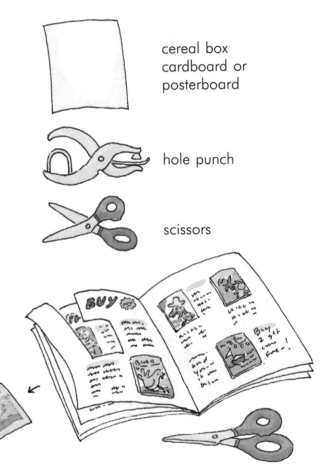

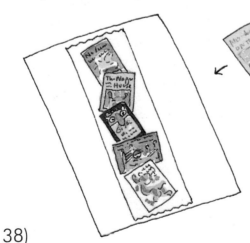

2 Glue the five pictures to the cardboard in a strip formation to make a bookmark. Let the glue dry, then cover the front of the bookmark area with clear packing tape to protect it.

3 Cut the bookmark out. Punch a hole in the top of the bookmark.

4 Cut an 8-inch (20-cm) piece of yarn. Thread the yarn through the hole and tie the two ends together leaving two 1-inch (2½-cm)-long ends. Cut two 2-inch (5-cm)-long pieces of yarn. Tie the two together in the center using the ends of the yarn on the bookmark. Unravel the yarn ends to make a tassel at the end of the bookmark.

Watch your school book club flyers for favorite titles to use in making your own personal bookmark.

When your friends see this owl, they'll want to know "Whoooo" made it!

Envelope Owl Wall Hanging

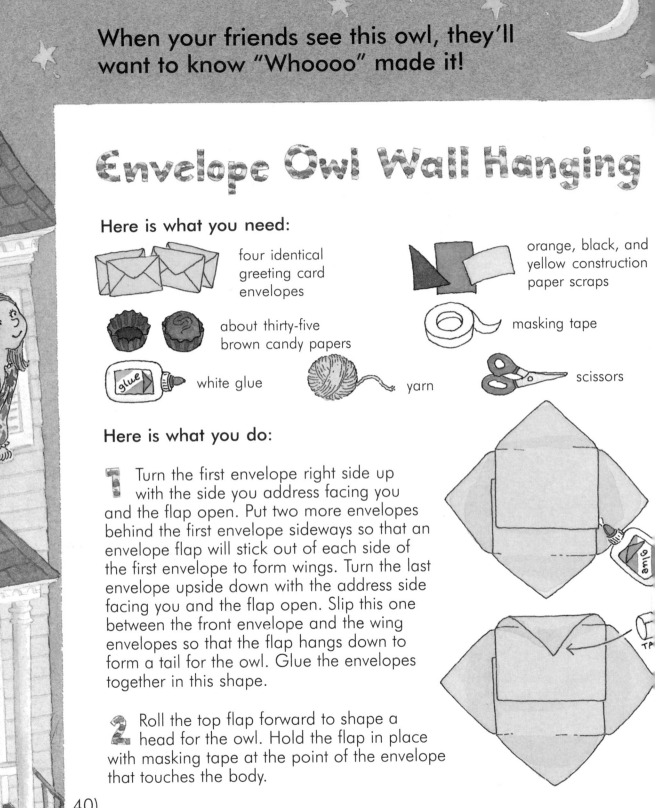

Here is what you need:

- four identical greeting card envelopes
- about thirty-five brown candy papers
- white glue
- orange, black, and yellow construction paper scraps
- masking tape
- yarn
- scissors

Here is what you do:

1. Turn the first envelope right side up with the side you address facing you and the flap open. Put two more envelopes behind the first envelope sideways so that an envelope flap will stick out of each side of the first envelope to form wings. Turn the last envelope upside down with the address side facing you and the flap open. Slip this one between the front envelope and the wing envelopes so that the flap hangs down to form a tail for the owl. Glue the envelopes together in this shape.

2. Roll the top flap forward to shape a head for the owl. Hold the flap in place with masking tape at the point of the envelope that touches the body.

3 Cut a triangle beak from the orange paper. Glue it in place over the masking tape on the point of the head. Cut eyes from the yellow and black paper and glue them in place above the beak. Cut two legs from the orange paper and glue them at the bottom of the body in front of the tail.

4 Cut fringe all the way around the edges of the wings and the tail.

5 Fold one third of the edge of a candy wrapper down to form two layers of pleats. Do this with all the wrappers, then glue them to the body and the tail of the owl for feathers.

6 Cut a 2-foot (60-cm)-long piece of yarn. Thread one end of the yarn through the fold of the owl's head and tie the two ends together to make a hanger. Cut a tiny slit on each side of the fold of the head flap. Slide the yarn into each slit to keep it from sliding.

If you used white envelopes instead of colored ones, you might want to color the owl with crayons or markers before you glue on the face, legs, and feathers.

41)

This pumpkin is so nice and squishy, you can use it for a pillow.

Soft Sculpture Pumpkin

Here is what you need:

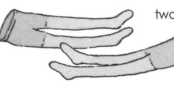 two pairs of old pantyhose

 orange and green poster paint and a paintbrush

 Styrofoam tray for drying

fiberfill

scissors

two rubber bands

stapler

Here is what you do:

1 Cut the four legs off the pantyhose. Arrange the legs crossing over each other at the center like the spokes of a wheel. Staple the legs together at the point where they all cross over each other.

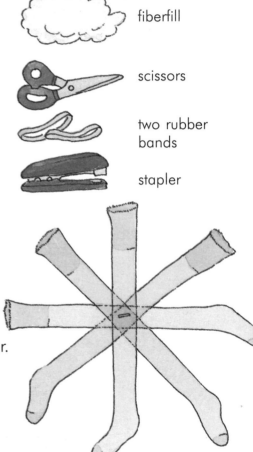

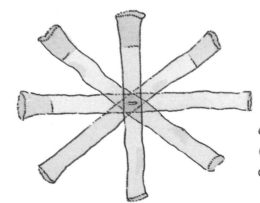

2 Cut the toe end off the foot of the pantyhose so that all the legs are open at the ends.

42)

3 Stuff all eight sections of pantyhose with fiberfill. Leave about 6 inches (15 cm) at the end of each stocking unstuffed.

4 Pull the eight sections up and around to the center to form a pumpkin. Hold the sections together with a rubber band.

5 Braid the excess stocking ends together to make a stem for the pumpkin. Hold the braided stem in place with another rubber band.

6 Paint the pumpkin orange and the stem green. Let the project dry on the Styrofoam tray.

You can turn this pumpkin into a jack-o'-lantern by gluing on a face cut from black felt.

Bat Finger Puppet

Here is what you need:

 black lipstick top or marker top

 black felt

 two small wiggle eyes

scrap of white rickrack

masking tape

scissors

white glue

black marker

Here is what you do:

FRONT   BACK

1 Put a small piece of masking tape on the top front of the tube to create a better gluing surface for the face and another on the back for the wings. Color the tape black with the marker.

2 Glue the two wiggle eyes on the taped part of the tube.

3 Cut two half points from the rickrack for teeth. Glue the teeth on below the eyes.

4 Cut two triangle ears from black felt. Glue the ears on the head of the bat above the eyes.

5 Cut wings for the bat from the black felt. Glue the wings over the tape at the back of the bat.

Slip your little bat friend over your finger and help him swoop for bugs.

Stuffed Black Cat

Here is what you need:

old black knit glove

old black sock

orange rickrack

two wiggle eyes

yellow yarn

stapler

masking tape

scissors

white glue

clamp clothespins

fiberfill

Here is what you do:

1 Stuff the hand of the black glove with fiberfill to make the body of the cat. If the cuff of the glove is more than 1 inch (2½ cm) long, cut off the extra cuff. Turn the rest of the cuff down into the glove and glue it in place. Use clamp clothespins to hold the opening shut while the glue dries.

46)

2 Cut a 3-inch (8-cm) piece from the toe end of the sock. Trim the cut end into two points to make ears on the head of the cat. Stuff the head with fiberfill. Staple the front and the back of the head together in a pleat between the ears.

3 The thumb of the glove is the tail of the cat. Glue a piece of rickrack across the tip of each finger to make the claws on the end of each leg. Glue a point of rickrack on each ear.

4 Put a piece of masking tape on the back of each wiggle eye and on the head where you will be gluing the eyes. This will create a better gluing surface and help the eyes to stay on the cat longer. Glue the eyes in place.

5 Cut three 3-inch (8-cm) pieces of yarn. Knot them together at the center. Fray the yarn ends to make whiskers. Trim the ends to make them even on both sides. Glue the whiskers to the face of the cat.

Meow! Meow! This is cat talk for "Happy Halloween."

Spider Paperweight

Here is what you need:

 two black knit gloves

pipe cleaners

 masking tape

4-inch (10-cm) rock

scissors

 two large wiggle eyes

white glue

Here is what you do:

1 Push the thumb of each glove inside the glove.

2 Cut eight 2½-inch (6-cm) pieces of pipe cleaner. Put a piece in each finger of the two gloves. Bend each finger to form a knee and foot of a spider leg.

3 Put the rock inside one of the gloves. If there is a lot of extra cuff, just fold it under the rock.

4 Slip the second glove over the first one, with the fingers on the other side of the rock so that there are four legs on each side of the rock. Turn any extra cuff back inside the glove.

5 Put a piece of masking tape on the back of each eye and on the front of the spider where the eyes will be glued. This helps to create a better gluing surface between the eyes and the glove. Glue the eyes in place.

Eek! A giant spider!

HAPPY HALLOWEEN

49)

Migrating Goose Finger Puppet

Here is what you need:

cardboard egg carton

golf tee

old knit glove

black and white poster paint and a paintbrush

scissors

fiberfill

white glue

masking tape

Styrofoam tray to work on

Here is what you do:

1 Cut three attached sections from the egg carton. The center cup section is the body of the goose and the two outer cups are the wings.

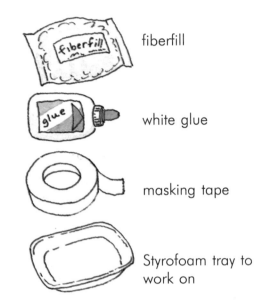

2 Poke the point of the golf tee through the center cup from the inside so that it sticks out to form a head for the goose. Use masking tape to tape the cup of the golf tee to the inside of the cup.

3 Cut a finger from the glove. Glue the finger into the center cup section with the opening sticking out from the back of the goose. Glue fiberfill over the glove finger inside the cup to make a fluffy breast for the bird.

4 Paint the head of the goose black and white and the body gray with dabs of black on the front of the wings. Squeeze the front and back of the two wing sections together while the paint is wet, so that they dry with a narrower shape than the body.

Good-bye, geese! See you next spring!

Let your teddy bear join with all the animals preparing for the cold weather.

Teddy Bear Cave

Here is what you need:

 large brown grocery bag

 white glue

scissors

 fiberfill

white paper

marker

stapler

Here is what you do:

1 Cut about 4 inches (10 cm) off the top of the grocery bag.

2 Cut an arched cave opening from one side of the bag.

3 Fold the two sides of the bag together and fold 1 inch (2½ cm) of the edge over. Staple along the edge to hold the fold in place.

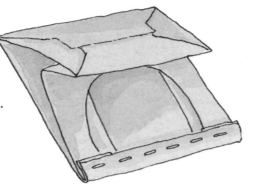

4 Pop the bag open to form a cave for your teddy bear to winter in. Glue some fiberfill snow along the top of the cave and along the bottom opening.

5 Make a sign for the cave that says Good night, Mr. Bear! See you in the spring! You might want to line the bottom of the cave with some dry leaves to make it comfy.

Goodnight Mr. Bear! See you in the spring!

Don't worry about not seeing your teddy bear for several months. Bears often wake up during the winter months and come out and wander around a little before going back to sleep.

Make this flag magnet in honor of Veteran's Day.

Flag Magnet

Here is what you need:

26 toothpicks

red marker

white glue

plastic lid for drying

scrap of blue construction paper

scissors

tiny gold star sequins or glitter

strip of sticky-backed magnet

Here is what you do:

1 Use the marker to color 14 toothpicks red.

2 Arrange them on the plastic lid starting with two red toothpicks across the top, then two natural colored toothpicks, alternating two of each color to make stripes of the flag. Our flag has 7 red stripes and 6 white ones.

3 Cover the toothpicks with a layer of white glue to hold them together. Do not flood the project with glue or the red marker will run.

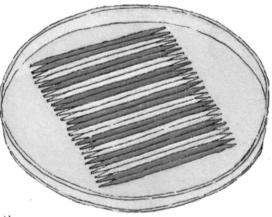

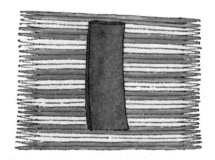

4 Cut a 1-inch (2½-cm) square of blue paper to glue on the upper left corner of the flag.

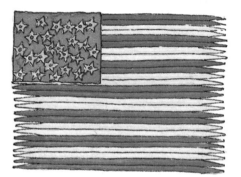

5 Cover the blue paper with glue and sprinkle it with the tiny stars. If you do not have stars you can dot the paper with glue then sprinkle it with glitter. You probably won't be able to fit all 50 stars on this tiny flag.

6 When the flag has dried completely peel the flag off the lid. Use scissors to trim off any excess glue.

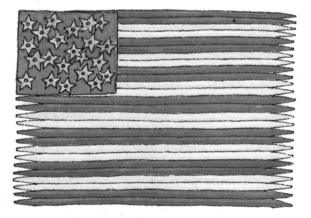

7 Stick a piece of sticky-back magnet on the back of the flag.

Put this flag on your refrigerator as a reminder of all the men and women who have served our country.

55)

Tennis Ball Turkey

Here is what you need:

old tennis ball

craft feathers

one bump of orange chenille-type pipe cleaner

two small wiggle eyes

buttons or corn kernels

brown poster paint and a paintbrush

paint stirrer stick

white glue

Styrofoam egg carton for drying

Here is what you do:

1 Ask an adult to cut a 1-inch (2½-cm) slit in the tennis ball.

2 Squeeze the slit on each side to open the ball enough to drop in some buttons or corn kernels to make the ball a shaker. Slide the end of the paint stirrer into the cut so that the shaker has a handle. Paint the ball brown.

56)

3 Bend the end of the orange bump chenille down to form a turkey head. Glue the head to the front of the ball. Glue the two wiggle eyes on each side of the head.

4 Glue colorful craft feathers across the back of the turkey for tail feathers.

5 Glue a craft feather on each side of the turkey for wings.

When the glue has dried, your turkey will be ready to shake in time to your favorite Thanksgiving songs.

57)

Make some ears of corn to celebrate the fall harvest.

Bubble Wrap Dried Corn

Here is what you need:

 cardboard paper towel tube

small bubbles bubble wrap

yellow and brown tissue paper

 masking tape

scissors

white glue

two Styrofoam trays

plastic spoon for mixing

newspaper to work on

Here is what you do:

1 Cut three 2-inch (5-cm) slits, evenly spaced, around one end of the tube. Wrap the cuts tightly over each other to form a point at the end of the tube. Use masking tape to hold the point together.

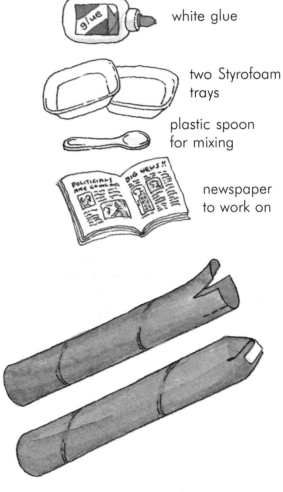

2 Wrap the entire tube in bubble wrap with the bubbles facing out. Tuck the extra wrap at each end of the tube down into

the tube. Use small pieces of masking tape to hold the wrap in place if you need to. It is important not to cover up the bubbles, which will form the kernels of corn.

3 Mix one part water with two parts glue in one of the Styrofoam trays. Roll the bubble wrap covered tube in the mixture, then cover it by wrapping it in two or three layers of yellow tissue paper. Tuck the excess paper at each end down into the tube.

4 Cut several long brown husks from the brown tissue paper. Glue them inside the tube at the wide end of the corncob.

5 Let the ear of corn dry completely on a Styrofoam tray.

This corn would look great with your Soft Sculpture Pumpkin and Stuffed Apples as a Thanksgiving centerpiece or hanging from the Sukkah for the Jewish holiday of Sukkot.

59)

These pilgrims work well as party hats or table decorations.

PARTY HAT PILGRIMS

Here is what you need:

two old cone-shaped party hats

black poster paint and a paintbrush

white, black, blue, yellow, and skin-colored construction paper

yarn in a hair color

white ribbon

markers

scissors

white glue

newspaper to work on

Here is what you do:

1 Paint the two party hats black and let them dry.

2 Cut two 3- by 4-inch (8- by 10-cm) rectangles of white paper for collars. Fold each collar in half and cut a neck hole. Slide each collar over the point of one hat and down about 1 inch (2½ cm). Cut a narrow triangle from the front of each collar.

3 Cut two 2-inch (5-cm) circles from the skin-colored paper for the heads. Draw a boy's face on one and a girl's face on the other with markers. Glue a head to the point of each hat above the collar.

4 Cut rectangle arms from the black paper for each pilgrim. Cut a white paper cuff to glue to the end of each arm. Cut hands from the skin-colored paper to glue at the end of each cuff. Glue the top of each arm to one side of each pilgrim.

5 To finish the girl pilgrim: Cut a rectangle of white paper for an apron and glue it to the front of the girl pilgrim. Cut three 1- by 2-inch (2½- by 5-cm) rectangles. Glue one on each side of the head, tipped out slightly, and one at the top of the head to form a bonnet. Tie a bow with the white ribbon and glue it at the chin. Glue on snips of yarn for hair.

6 To finish the boy pilgrim: Cut a belt from the blue paper and a belt buckle from the yellow paper. Glue them in place across the front of the boy pilgrim. Cut a hat from the black construction paper and glue it on the head. Decorate the hat with a belt and buckle cut from the blue and yellow paper. Cut some snips of yarn to glue on for hair.

What a charming pair of pilgrims!

61)

The cornucopia is a symbol of the plentiful food that we give thanks for at Thanksgiving time.

Cornucopia Place Cards

Here is what you need:

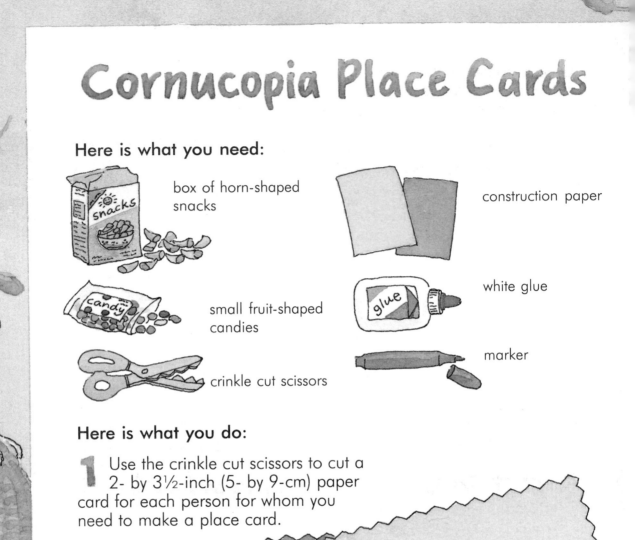

box of horn-shaped snacks

construction paper

small fruit-shaped candies

white glue

crinkle cut scissors

marker

Here is what you do:

1 Use the crinkle cut scissors to cut a 2- by 3½-inch (5- by 9-cm) paper card for each person for whom you need to make a place card.

2 Glue a horn-shaped snack in the top left-hand corner of each card for a cornucopia.

3 Glue three or four little candies spilling out of the horn.

Kathy

Daniel

Sarah

Use the marker to write the name of each guest on a place card.

About the Author and Artist

Twenty years as a teacher and director of nursery school programs in Oneida, New York, have given Kathy Ross extensive experience in guiding children through craft projects. A collector of teddy bears and paper dolls, her craft projects have frequently appeared in *Highlights* magazine. She is the author of The Millbrook Press's Holiday Crafts for Kids series, including *Crafts for Halloween*, *Crafts for Christmas*, and *Every Day Is Earth Day*. She is also the author of *Gifts to Make for Your Favorite Grown-ups*, *The Best Holiday Craft Book Ever*, *Crafts for Kids Who Are Wild About Dinosaurs*, and *Crafts for Kids Who Are Wild About Outer Space*.

A resident of Andover, Massachusetts, Vicky Enright studied editorial design/illustration at Syracuse University. To date, she has utilized her talents as a calligrapher, a wallpaper designer, and a greeting-card illustrator. Her first book was *Crafts From Your Favorite Fairy Tales* by Kathy Ross. She is the illustrator of the other three season books in this series: *Crafts to Make in the Spring*, *Crafts to Make in the Summer*, and *Crafts to Make in the Winter*.